# IKWA OF THE TEMPLE MOUNDS

*Ikwa and her friend work hard grinding
corn and nuts or shell.*

# IKWA
# OF THE
# TEMPLE
# MOUNDS

Margaret Zehmer Searcy

**The University of Alabama Press**
University, Alabama

Copyright © 1974 by
The University of Alabama Press
ISBN 0–8173–4000–9
Library of Congress Catalog Card Number 74–2814
Manufactured in the United States of America

# contents

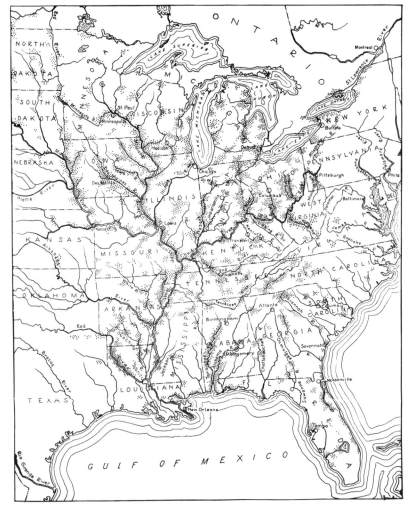

*Map of mound locations in the Eastern United States.*

# The Priest's Command

The tattooed old priest stood on the top of the big temple mound. He looked very fierce. He was painted red and white. His big headdress was made of feathers, deer antlers, and copper. The dancing fire in the temple doorway caused his copper and mica ornaments to shine. They seemed to move and looked as though they were alive.

He spoke to a child in a deep voice, "The sun looked weak today. You must bring the sun god a sacrifice in the morning." Then he gave a second command: "You are old enough to start learning the secrets of our people. You must know where and when they lived, their life ways, and what they believed. The curse of ignorance will be upon you if you don't learn."

This priest might have said these things to you if you had lived in the Southeastern United States over eight hundred years ago. You would have been an Indian because no one was there but Indians. If you were a girl your name might have been Ikwa. If you were Ikwa's brother you were called Situ.

Your people were not savages. They were farmers. Their fields were found up and down the rivers and streams all over the Southeast. You did not live in a tepee. You lived in a house in a typical village. The people in your village had built a huge earthen mound on which to put a temple. Your village was built around a public square, like a park. Here games were played and dances were held. The town elders met in a council house to make rules for the village. Sometimes the chief elders traveled to bigger towns to make agreements for many towns. There were many villages and mounds built along the Mississippi River and its tributaries, and today all your people are called the Mississippi Temple Mound Builders. Mounds are found in many of the Southeastern states today, but the Mississippi way of life disappeared about four hundred years ago.

Your people were happy people, but your Mississippi Indian ways were not like the ways of modern people. Mississippi Indians had never seen a horse, or used a wheel, or learned to smelt metal. Everyone believed in many gods and spirits, both bad and good—even a rattlesnake god! Parents believed that bad spirits got inside of children and made them misbehave. Bad children had to be cut with a sharp stone or scratched with a snake fang to let the evil spirit come out.

You can see why Ikwa and Situ would try to be good. They would not want to be cut or scratched. If you are pretending that you are Ikwa or Situ, this book will help you to obey the priest's second command. It will teach you some of the secrets of the Indians.

The Priest had said to learn how the Indians lived. Modern scientists have made it possible for us to know these things. All the material objects described in the story really did exist. Many of these can be seen in museums. Some children even find Indian tools in their own backyards.

Of course, this story is about a time before people learned to write in this part of the world. The customs in the story are described in the writings of early explorers and visitors who saw some of the descendants of these people. We can't say that this story really did happen, but it is based upon a lot of facts. We can't say that it absolutely couldn't have happened. Read the story and see what you think. . . . But first you might like to meet the people in the story:

IKWA'S FAMILY

**Ikwa** (ĭk'wä): A girl of twelve who is learning to be a woman.

**Situ** (sĭt' oō): Ikwa's older brother who is hoping to win an important game.

**Ikwa's Mother:** A member of the Alligator Clan.

**Ikwa's Grandmother:** Her mother's mother. She teaches Ikwa the things an Alligator member should know.

**Ikwa's Father:** A member of the Eagle Clan.

**Lowe** (lō'wē): Ikwa's mother's younger sister.

KOMA'S FAMILY

**Koma** (kō'mä): Situ's cousin and best friend.

**Inna** (ĭn'nä): Koma's little six-year-old sister who has to care for the baby.

**Her Baby Brother:** A little boy who is still bound to a cradle board.

**Koma's Father:** A member of the Eagle Clan who is sad because his wife has been killed by a snake.

OTHER IMPORTANT CHARACTERS

**The Priest:** The leader of the village who guides the people in making important decisions.

**The Trader:** A crafty man who carries goods and gossip from one village to the next. He is a member of the Skunk Clan.

**Noha** (nō′hä): Ikwa's future husband. He and Ikwa have never seen each other.

**Rata** (rä′tä): Noha's mother, a member of the Eagle Clan.

**Sinu** (sĭn′yoō): A girl who lives in Ikwa's village.

2

*The priest in the temple with some of the men conduct a "new fire" ceremony.*

# 1

# The Sun's Breakfast

A frightening thing was happening to Ikwa this morning. For the first time in her life, she was starting the long climb up the log steps that led to the temple on top of the man-made mound. She was taking the sun his breakfast. It was still dark, but far above her a flickering fire guided her. The old priest stood in the open side of the temple by the fire.

Last week the old priest had said, "Ikwa, you are getting old enough to learn the ways of a woman. Soon you will have lived twelve summers. You should begin by learning to serve the gods. I have talked to your parents. At the time of the next new moon take that pretty basket that you are weaving and fill it full of the corn, squash, and beans that you and the women have grown. Bring it to the temple before dawn as an offering to the sun god."

She had been so excited when he said this that she had trembled. Was it possible that the priest thought she was old enough to be a woman? Was it possible that she might be old enough to be chosen to take the long journey down the river to the festival at the Holy Place of All Gods?

3

Priests wore headdresses made in many ways. The copper
ornaments on this one gleam in the firelight.

How proud Ikwa had been when the priest had spoken to her. How cold and frightened she was today. Her feet were wet from the dew. The fog from the river was wet. She shivered. She hoped that the moisture wouldn't fade the design of red, yellow, and brown vegetable dye on her new fringed apron. The girl and her mother had made it from the hide of a deer that her brother Situ had killed. They had decorated it with shell beads from the great sea far away. Today was the first time she had worn it, and she was proud of it.

Ikwa walked through a spider web. It stuck to her forehead and clung across her nose. She rubbed her face on her bare shoulder trying to get the sticky strands off. She couldn't let go of the heavy basket to use her hands. She imagined she felt the spider crawling on her chin. She almost fell as she stepped to the next log. There were only forty-two steps leading to the flat top of the mound, but Ikwa felt as though there were thousands. Something damp and slimy brushed her ankle in the dark. She shuddered, "What could it be? Could it be a snake? Is a snake god living under one of these logs? Will he come out and bite my bare foot?" She drew up her toes.

Ikwa knew that a snake with a white mouth had bitten her cousin Koma's mother last spring. The priest made strong magic and sang his best songs to cure her, but the power of the snake god was too strong. Two days later, Koma's mother was dead. Ikwa's father helped Koma and his father dig her grave in the floor of their house. They buried their loved one in their home to keep her spirit close to them. Ikwa and her mother tried to comfort Koma's little sister, Inna, who was only six. They helped her care for her baby brother.

Ikwa was terrified as she stood in the dark, listening

**4**

*The log steps.*

**5**

*How Ikwa's village looked. These figures are not real Indians but are made of wax.*

for snake noises. She heard the breath of the wind blowing the wet grass, and the feeding chatter of one old mallard duck on the river. Noises were louder in the fog. Then a new noise made her jump, "Aaaooo, aaaooo, aaaooo, aaaooo!" Four terrible howls shut out all the other noises. This was the call of the priest to wake his elder brother, the sun. Then his deep voice spoke to Ikwa:

"Hurry, child, the sun must have his morning food. He must be strong for his long trip across the sky. He must use his life-giving warmth to make the crops grow. We don't have much time."

Ikwa hastened up the last few steps. With trembling hands she gave him her basket. They walked to the fire together. She was relieved to be with him in the light, though he still looked very fierce. His copper ear spools shone like two big eyes. His headdress was made of deer antlers and copper, and he wore a cape of feathers. His mica and copper ornaments danced in the firelight.

The old man sang some strange holy words and held her basket above the fire. Two ears of corn, a few beans, and a squash fell into the fire. Soon little flames jumped from one ear of corn to the other. The beans were gone with a flash. The squash sputtered and spewed, sending smoke into the sky.

"Look, child, the sun has accepted your gift. He is awaking from his long night's sleep."

She watched as the sun stretched and made the darkness run. His long fingers, golden sunbeams, lit the straw roof of the temple. They shone on the carved wooden masks of the other gods above it. The mask of the alligator was higher than the others. The alligator was the special god of Ikwa's people.

"Long ago," said the priest, "the alligator came to

*How Koma and Situ smoked meat for the winter supply.*

10

earth in the form of a man. He was the father of the first man in this village."

The fog was disappearing, and the sun shone on the thatched roofs of the twelve houses below. How tiny they looked! Ikwa had never seen the whole village at the same time before. She could see all of the strong log wall that ran around the village and down to the river. The wall protected the people from the wild animals of the forest, from evil spirits, and from enemies in times of war.

A gentle breeze was blowing from the river. The river looked calm and peaceful now. Ikwa knew that there would be times when the heavens would cry. The river would become angry. He would send his waters over his banks, and he would take everything that he wanted. The river was a friend, though. He always left a present of new soil in the fields he had flooded. The rich soil, abundant rains, and warm sun made the crops grow.

Ikwa saw Koma and Situ come out of their houses. Last night they had had a quarrel. Koma had made a new fishhook out of the ankle bone of a deer. He wanted to try it out. Situ had wanted to go hunting. Situ had liked hunting better than fishing ever since he had lost his father's copper fishhook. His father had gotten the hook from a trader from the north. Situ hoped that he could get a new one for his father one day. He didn't like to use a net with stone sinkers. He didn't want to make a shell or bone hook.

Koma had said, "Situ, we went hunting last. It is my turn to choose what we do tomorrow. I am tired of eating rabbit and deer. I want some fish."

Situ had answered, "You always get your way, Koma. It is my turn to win an argument."

Ikwa knew now who had won. She saw Koma and Situ push her father's dugout canoe into the river. Then she

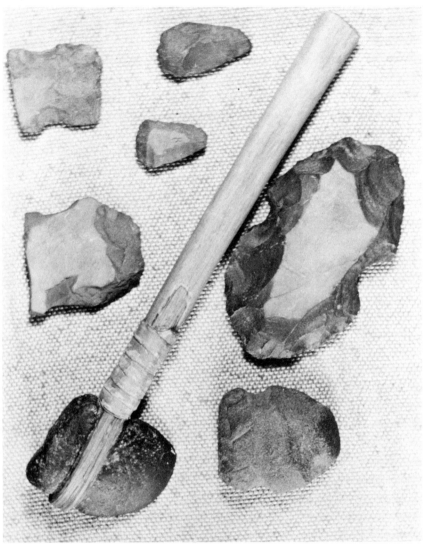

*Koma and Situ used stone axes to clear the forests. Then Ikwa and her mother used the other stones to make hoes or pointed tools for working the ground and for planting seeds.*

saw her father and the other men going toward the forest. They were going to clear new land for next spring's crops. The men would use the stone axes to cut the bark in a circle around the big trees. The trees would die and would be burned later. The men would save the small, straight logs to use in the village. Some would be used in the village wall. Some would be used in building houses.

Ikwa dreamed of having a house of her own. That time would come when her promised husband, Noha, would leave the Eagle Village to live in her village. A husband always moved to his bride's home to live. She wondered what Noha was like. She had never seen him. Her marriage had been arranged by the village elders.

Ikwa was sad when she remembered that soon Koma and Situ would get married and leave. Their marriage would take place after the ceremony of a Good Harvest at the Holy Place of All Gods. Certain women from her clan would go to help build the houses for the new families.

"I really want to grow up," thought Ikwa. "If only I could be chosen to help. I do wish that Situ and Koma could live here forever. I don't want them to move away."

She stopped daydreaming when she heard the voice of the old priest speaking to her, "Look, the gods have been pleased. They have sent you a sign. See the birds? We are going to have a visit from a stranger soon."

Ikwa saw that two crows and a hawk had been awakened by the morning sun. The three birds were flying toward the village. Hawks and crows were mutual enemies, and it was unusual for them to fly together. This was truly a sign of the gods! Who could the stranger be?

The girl started down the steep steps to the village. Now, in the sunlight, they were not scary at all. "How silly I've been to be afraid," she said to herself. She jumped over

13

*Koma and Situ decide not to use the fish net and the fish trap.*
*Koma wants to try out his new fishhook in the river.*

8b

the last three logs and ran to tell her mother of the sign. "If the boys catch some fish, I'll take some to the priest," she thought.

Her mother handed her a cornmeal cake and some cold rabbit meat and smiled at her.

"Ikwa, the sun must have liked his breakfast. He is so strong and warm this morning. Did he send you a sign?"

"Mother, we must get ready. Enemies flew together toward this village—two crows and a hawk! The priest says that a stranger is coming. I wonder who he will be."

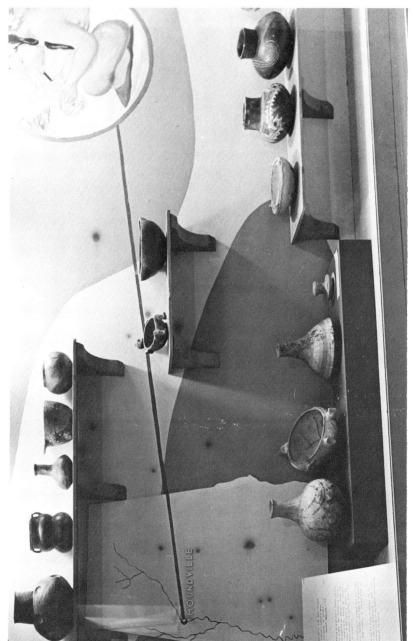

Ikwa's people knew how to make pots of many sizes and shapes.

9

16

# 2

# A Spirit Pot and
# Grown-People's Secrets

Ikwa and her mother were going to make pottery this morning. Ikwa liked to make pottery. What fun she and Koma and Situ had had getting the good clay from the riverbank yesterday. The river had given them the mussel shells, too. They would grind the shells and mix them with the clay to make it strong and keep it from cracking. Ikwa's mother interrupted her thoughts:

"Ikwa, take off your new clothes. Take my corn grinder and grind the shells while I beat the clay and get the rocks and sticks out. But first go and ask little Inna if she wants us to watch the baby while we work." Ikwa ran next door and spoke to the small girl.

Since Inna's mother had died it had been her job to take care of her little brother. He wasn't much trouble because he was still strapped to the cradle board. He was a cute fat baby, who was just beginning to learn to talk. He had been nearly eight months old when his mother died, old enough to eat vegetables. So he had lived. Inna brought the baby and hung his cradle on a tree limb. Then she ran off to play with the other small girls in the village.

Ikwa changed her clothes. She put on her only other apron. How ragged it looked compared with her new one. There was a big, ugly grease spot right on the front. It had no shell beads. She and her mother had cut all of them off of it to sew on the new apron.

"It won't matter too much if I get clay on it," she thought. She peeped around the tree at the baby and saw him smiling. Then she started to crack the shells.

"Hurry, daughter, we have so much work to do. You know these pots will have to dry several days before we can fire them. It is so dry now that a week's time should be more than enough. I promised the priest that I would teach you how to make a special alligator bowl. It is for the dead to take to the spirit world. The priest always keeps some of these bowls in the temple. I have been saving bear grease for weeks."

"Mother, how do you make the beautiful black glaze on the spirit bowls?"

"This is a secret of our people. Now that you are old enough to take offerings to the temple, I will tell you. These pots need to be dark so they can carry food into the world of the dead." Her mother handed Ikwa the powdery clay to mix with the shells. Then the woman poured some water into the dry mixture and the two began to mix, knead, and work it. Next they rolled it on the smooth rock into long snakelike pieces. Then they coiled these around until they formed the shapes they wanted. Each took turns using a slick rock to smooth the sides. "Ikwa," her mother said, "to make a black finish requires an extra step. When it is dry, I will place it carefully in the fire and cover it with slow-burning grasses, as I do with all pots. When it is hot, I will take it out of the fire with a bent green stick. I will dip it into melted bear grease and then fire it again with dried plant material.

18

*The alligator was a special god of Ikwa's people.*

The spirit of the dead bear makes his beautiful shiny black color come on the pot."

They looked up when they heard the happy cooing of the baby. A pretty girl several years older than Ikwa had come up to the young child. The two of them were playing a baby "peep" game. The girl was Ikwa's mother's younger sister, Lowe. She was the aunt of Inna, Koma, and the baby, the three children whose mother the snake had killed.

"Tell Inna to get the baby at my house," the girl said. "I have cooked some soft beans for him. I have something for Inna, too. I made a new red sash for her on my loom. Don't tell her, though. I want to see her face when it surprises her." She lovingly took his cradle from the tree and started down the path.

As soon as she was out of sight, Ikwa's mother said, "I'll tell you a grown people's secret. Last night the village elders decided that Lowe would marry the baby's father. She loves her sister's children. Who else would make them a better mother than Lowe? They will marry when the song of sadness is gone from the heart of the father. He is a good man. They will be happy, and his children will be happy again." Ikwa thought about this for a moment, and she smiled at her mother.

All that week Ikwa and her mother made pottery. The spirit pot was made in the shape of an alligator bowl. They made pots for the family and some extra pots to use for trading. Some pots were rounded on the bottom to sit on three rocks in the fire. Other pots had little legs. Ikwa drew designs on some while the clay was still moist. They pinched some of the sides with their fingers and poked others with a stick or bone. A pot with a rough outer surface wouldn't slip out of a person's hands so easily as a smooth one. She put tiny strap handles on a few.

20

*Lowe weaves clothing on her loom. She has made a new red sash for Inna.*

This piece of woven cloth, decorated with shell beads, was found next to a copper ornament at Etowah, Georgia. It was made hundreds of years ago by Ikwa's people out of vegetable fibers.

Ikwa brushed her hair out of her eyes. A streak of mud was left on her cheek. Then she carefully made the magic marks that her grandmother had taught her. Her people had no schools. Her mother and the other Alligator women taught the girls everything they should know.

Her mother was making a squatty little paint pot. It was shaped like a frog. Ikwa was making a fat round pot. It had a funny head for one handle and feet and legs for the other.

Suddenly her mother spoke: "What is wrong with the dogs? Listen to them bark and growl. Go and look toward the river. See if you can see anyone, Ikwa. Don't worry about the pots; you can scratch figures on them after they are baked."

Ikwa went and hid behind a tree overlooking the path. She saw Koma and Situ coming down the path bringing a string of fish. A tall stranger was following them. He was enormous. His loin cloth was tied below a big roll of fat around his middle. It jiggled with every step he took. He looked hot and dirty and tired. By his many tattooes Ikwa knew that he was an important man. A red scar cut through the design on his chest. The rows of tattooing no longer matched because of the scar. The worst thing about the man was the look in his eyes. He looked as if he didn't like anything he saw.

One of the friendlier puppies ran up to him, wagging its tail, and sniffed him. The man hit the dog cruelly with a stick. The puppy ran off limping and howling in pain.

After the three were out of sight, Ikwa went back to her mother. "There is a stranger with Koma and Situ. He is old, ugly, and mean. I wonder who he is?"

The man was old, ugly, and mean.

# 3

# The Mystery
# of the Stranger

The big man was the first stranger that the Alligator People had seen in over thirty days. Ikwa's father and the other men came from the fields. They greeted the man. Ikwa couldn't quite hear what they said, but she thought she heard the words, "Eagle Village."

"Why, Noha lives there!" she remembered.

Ikwa and her mother and the other women stayed where they were. Some of the women were still in the fields. But all the men and older boys went with the stranger to the top of the big mound to greet the priest.

"Ikwa," her mother spoke sharply, "Go and get the fish off the stump where Situ left them. The dogs may eat them if you don't. We must go and cook for the men and our guest. Go and get one of our new pots. Be careful; don't burn your fingers. They are still hot from firing."

Ikwa obeyed. She knew that her mother was talking fast to keep from thinking about why the stranger had come. The last time a stranger had come, he took several of the young men from the village with him. They had gone to the Place of All Gods to labor on the mounds that were being

*Ikwa is taught to make pottery by her mother while her grandfather watches.*

made as temple bases. New mounds were being built, and old ones were being made larger. The priests said that it was an honor to serve the gods this way, but war captives did the same work. The last stranger had carried away many baskets of food to feed the mound builders and priests. Now all the men who were left in the Alligator Village were needed to help harvest the crops. There would be enough food in the village to last through the winter, but there was not much to spare. Ikwa's mother was afraid that her father and Situ would have to go. Everyone knew that he must obey the priests and serve the gods if he were asked. The gods would be angry with him if he didn't. But the Alligator Village was small, and there were many other villages scattered up and down the river. Perhaps the Alligator men wouldn't be asked.

"Hurry, Ikwa, put on your new clothes and wash the clay off your face and hands. You must help me fix the food and carry it up to the men. The other women won't be here to help us. They must finish getting the corn from the fields. They must gather it if we are to eat this winter. The crows and raccoons are about to eat all of it. We probably should have helped them, but we needed to make the pots. Besides, someone needed to stay here to cook."

Ikwa was proud to be asked to take the food to the men's meeting. She had never been to a men's meeting. She ran to the cool spring to wash. She looked at her serious face and smooth black hair in the mirror made by the quiet water. She rubbed the mud off her cheek and looked again. She liked what she saw. "If the stranger knows Noha, maybe he will tell him what a pretty girl his future wife is," she thought. She smiled at the face in the water.

Then a strange thing happened. A dragonfly flew down and hit the surface of the water. The ripples in the

*Situ brings in a big basket of corn for the women to cook.*
*Green corn is his favorite.*

water made little wrinkles of worry, which spread over the face pictured there. Could this be a bad omen? Would something bad happen to Ikwa?

Then Ikwa had a terrible thought, "Could the mean old stranger be Noha? If he is Noha, I don't want to take the food to the men's meeting. I don't want to climb the steps to the top of the mound. If he is Noha, I pray that a snake god will crawl out and kill me. I couldn't stand to be married to a man like him. He would beat me just like he beat the dog."

Ikwa wanted to run away and hide. Instead, she slowly walked back to the house. She changed her apron and went to join her mother.

"Hurry, Ikwa, we must take this food up while it is hot. We don't want the stranger to think that the Alligator women are so slow that their men have to eat cold food."

Her mother handed her a bowl, being careful not to spill the steaming food. They walked slowly up the long stairway. No snake was around any of the logs. Quietly they walked into the temple.

The men were sitting in a circle smoking, passing the pipe from one man to the next. She watched her brother Situ take the pipe. He took a puff and turned red in the face, trying not to cough. He took one more puff on the pipe and passed it to Koma. Ikwa turned and looked at the stranger. He was even uglier than she had remembered and, yes, he looked very mean. If he were Noha, she would die. Ikwa and her mother served each man. When she served her father, he smiled a secret smile at her.

The priest picked up the ceremonial cups made of big shells, which had come from the ocean many days' journey away. He put a strange black drink of herbs into each cup and passed one to each man. The priest motioned to the women to leave. Ikwa and her mother started the long climb back down the mound.

When they got to the bottom, all the girls and the women of the village were waiting to question them:

"Who is the stranger? Will the men and boys have to go with him? Will we have to give him our food? What does he want? Why did he come?"

Ikwa and her mother did not know the answers to these questions, so the women and children decided to go to bed. The men might talk all night.

Ikwa was too worried to go to sleep right away. Hours went by while she listened to the owls and crickets talking to one another. She heard the whippoorwill calling his mate. An owl answered far away in the swamp. "A whippoorwill's mate is pretty," she thought. "Birds and crickets and animals are so lucky; they can choose their mates." Finally she fell asleep.

*Shell cups, this pipe, and bowl were used by the men in the temple.*

*Ikwa dreamed that a tattooed snake held her prisoner.*

# 4

# A Bad Bargain

Ikwa slept poorly that night. Once she cried out in her sleep. She dreamed she was held prisoner by a fat tattooed snake who had two heads. The snake held a big stick in his tail. He was trying to beat her with it. He was making a strange noise.

Ikwa woke up. The only noise she heard was the noise of an angry bluejay. It was scolding someone who had dared to come close to its nest in the tree outside. Ikwa opened her eyes and looked around the room. Her mother and father were gone. Her brother Situ lay sleeping on a straw mat on the other side of the fire hearth. The sun was coming through the doorway. The gods of the darkness had been chased away. Ikwa lay still a few minutes. She hated to get up. Her back ached. She had a cramp in her foot. She felt tired, even though it was late in the morning. Then she remembered. "The stranger?"

"Wake up, Situ." She got up and hurried across the room and shook her brother. He would know who the visitor was. Situ turned over and muttered something hateful. When he was sleepy, he sometimes said ugly things

33

to Ikwa, even though he shouldn't. Situ had stayed awake most of the night with the other men talking to the stranger. He didn't want to be bothered now. Ikwa knew better than to shake him again.

The bird was still sounding its shrill "jay" cry. Ikwa peeped through a hole in the mud and wattle wall of the house. She wanted to see what was disturbing the bird. The ugly stranger was sitting under the nesting tree. He was talking to her father and her mother's two brothers. Her mother was smiling and giving the men leftover stew and corn cakes. She was using some of the new pots. Ikwa moved to the doorway, trying to hear what they were saying. She couldn't quite hear the stranger. Then her uncle spoke, "Yes, we will give you the spirit bowl and ten of our best pots for a copper fishhook."

Ikwa was frightened and angry. "How can my uncles give that horrid old man my bowls? They are the best bowls I ever made. They don't know how hard pottery is to make. The spirit bowl is just beautiful. Who is that old man anyway? Are my uncles using my own bowls for my marriage gifts? Does the stranger think that I am worth only one copper fishhook?"

The stranger said something in a low voice. Then Ikwa's uncle spoke again, "I will give you six baskets of corn for a block of your best soapstone and two conch shell cups. I want to carve a new stone pipe for our priest. Soon Koma and Situ will be men, and they will need ceremonial cups. No, you don't want corn? Then I'll trade you a beaver hide and two soft deerskins. I'll even throw in a length of woven cloth. This is all we have. Yes, we need more salt, but we will have to wait. We'll get it from you at the festival market next month. I will find some good flint to trade by then."

Ikwa was so relieved that she felt dizzy. She leaned

*How the men's meeting looked.*

18

35

against the rough wall to keep from falling. This man was the new trader. He didn't want her for his wife. Her relatives weren't exchanging marriage gifts with him. No wonder Situ was cross this morning. He must have stayed up all night listening to the news of the other villages up and down the river. The trader traveled hundreds of miles in his big dugout canoe. He took goods and gossip from one village to the other. Listening to traders had taught her that there were big towns with many mounds—some large, some small, and some in the shapes of animals. Certain villages were very rich. Their priests rode in litters carried by other men. A few men were so rich and important that they had several wives. A trader saw many wonderful things. The last trader had told Situ of visiting the pigeon roosts to get birds and feathers. The birds came from the north in such great numbers that they darkened the sky.

No, this man couldn't be Noha. Noha wasn't a trader. He hunted and fished and cleared fields in the Eagle Village. Oh, wonderful day! Oh, happy day! She wouldn't have to marry this mean old man!

The jay swooped down and pecked at Ikwa's mother. Ikwa started to laugh. She giggled and laughed and shook until tears ran down her cheeks. She really wasn't laughing at the bird. She was laughing for relief and joy.

Situ opened one eye and said another hateful word. Situ felt terrible. He could still taste that bad black drink that he had had to drink with the men last night. Smoking hadn't agreed with him either. Ikwa took one look at his frowning face. She stopped laughing, tied on her old apron, and quickly went outside.

The trader looked up and spoke to her, "Good morning, young woman."

"Good morning, to you, sir. Do you travel to the

36

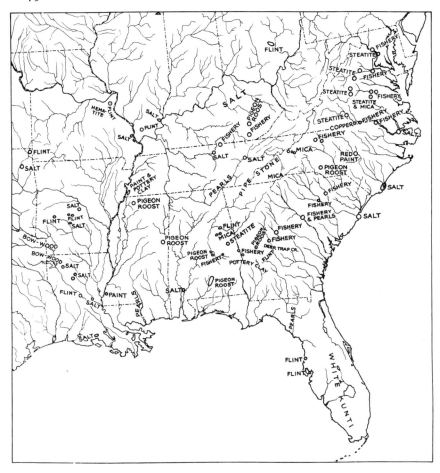

A map of natural resources used by the Indians
in the Southeast. The trader took them from
one village to the next.

Eagle Village? Do you know Noha?"

"Yes, I go there. I think I know Noha."

Ikwa's mother spoke, "Noha is the son of Rata and Nooga. Ikwa is promised to him. They will marry next year."

The trader nodded his head. "Oh, yes, I know him well." A half smile came on his face. He looked around and then spoke to Ikwa. "Ikwa, I'll trade you the answers to any two questions you ask for that pretty beaded apron you wore last night."

All Ikwa could think about was Noha, which meant that she really wasn't thinking at all. She forgot that an Indian girl has only two aprons. She forgot how precious the shell beads from the great sea were. She forgot how hard she and her mother had worked to make the apron. She forgot that she wanted to wear it when Noha saw her for the first time.

She ran to get the apron, shouting her questions as she went, "Is Noha old and ugly? Is he kind and brave?"

Ikwa returned with the apron in a few seconds. She handed it to the trader. Her mother and father looked shocked. Her father looked at her mother and started to say something. Her mother frowned and shook her head. Now that Ikwa had taken the offering to the sun she was supposed to be a woman. She was not to be treated as a child. Her parents said nothing.

The stranger smiled slightly and answered, "Noha is as old as the number of seasons that he has lived. He is as ugly as he looks and acts. He is as brave as his courage and as kind as his deeds. To know a man you must look into his mind. Now, I am taking this skirt, but not for the answers to your questions. I am taking it as payment for the valuable lesson I am teaching you. In the future, know what you want before you trade. Know what you are going to get. Consult your elders before you make a bargain. If you want to be a woman, you must act like one."

With these words the trader took the apron. Then he gathered up the other goods, nodded to her parents, and left.

Ikwa's father shook his head and said, "Oh, Ikwa, what have you done?"

Her mother spoke, "Leave the child alone. Having to wear that old, ragged apron and miss the festival will be punishment enough. I am ashamed of her. We just traded all of our extra hides and cloth. We don't have any material or beads to use for a new apron. I am not willing to help her get another new one anyway. I only hope that she has learned a lesson."

The bird swooped down again. Ikwa turned and ran down the hill to the spring—to sit, and cry, and think. "If Noha sees me in this ragged, muddy old apron he won't want me. He will think I am dirty and sloppy and lazy. I wouldn't want Situ to marry a thoughtless baby like me."

Ikwa's tears fell into the spring and spread ripples of worry over the troubled face reflected in the water. The dragonfly omen had come true.

*How Koma and Situ made their boat.*

*Koma's and Situ's new canoe. The river is their highway. They enjoy canoe races with other boys from the next village.*

40

# 5

## Frog Medicine
## and a Canoe

Koma and Situ came down the path. They noticed how sad Ikwa looked. Situ stopped and spoke to his sister, "Ikwa, I didn't mean to be so cross this morning. I didn't mean to hurt your feelings. I'm sorry. It is just that my stomach hurts and my head feels so heavy. I hope I'll feel better in a little while. I thought about going to see the priest to get him to make a little spell to cure me, but that takes too long."

"Don't believe him, Ikwa," said Koma. "Situ is afraid that the priest might not be able to suck the pain out with his medicine tube or frighten it with his rattles and chants. He might have to cut him with a flint knife or scratch him with a snake fang to let the pain out. If he doesn't do these things, he might give him some bitter herbs to drink. Situ drank too much of the priest's medicine and smoked too much tobacco last night. Situ isn't old enough to take a man's medicine without getting sick. Don't let anything he says make you cry."

"I'm not crying because of anything you said, Situ. I am crying because of what I said and did. I let that mean old

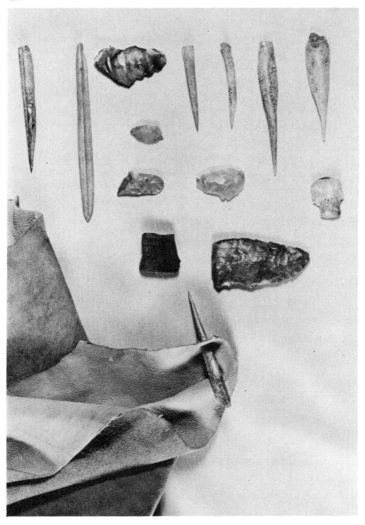

*Ikwa's sewing kit. Sharp bones were used to punch holes in the tough leather. When they became dull Ikwa sharpened them on her whetstone. The small thin flakes of stone were sharpened on one edge. She used these to cut hides. Other stones were not as sharp. She used them as skin scrapers or multipurpose tools. Ikwa always kept one big rough stone to cut extra thick, tough hides. Guess which stone she used as a thread cutter.*

trader trick me out of my only good clothes. Now I can't possibly go to the festival. If Noha sees me in these rags, he won't want me. No one would want a dirty, stupid bride."

"Oh, Ikwa," said her brother gently. "Save your tears until you really have something to cry about. You still have plenty of time to make another apron. We have a beaver pelt, two prime deer hides, and a length of woven cloth."

"No, we don't. The men traded them all for a copper fishhook and some shell cups for you," snapped the unhappy girl.

"Oh, Ikwa, I'm sorry you have problems. I would help you if I could. Gee, I'm sorry about the hides. I don't know what you can do. Maybe we can think of something. Why don't you bring our dinner to us, and Koma and I will try to think of something? Don't bring us any of the fish stew. I think the fish made me sick. Bring me some of the corn meal mush. Maybe later I'll feel more like eating. I sure don't want anything now."

"Why can't you get your dinner yourself. Why do I need to bring it to you?"

"Koma and I are going to start on our canoe today. You remember that great cypress tree, the one where the wild turkey roosted? We are going there. Koma and I cut a ring in the bark around it last fall. We left a stone axe by it, and every time we hunted there, we would cut a little more. We would hit the tree hard with it and then use a stone chisel to dig away the splintered wood."

"I know that," said Ikwa. "Is it ready now?"

"Oh, you watched us," said Situ. "Well, yesterday we burned the last part that held up the tree. It finally fell. Today we are going to cut or burn off the branches. We are going to set fire to the center part to make the inside hollow.

I borrowed one of your baskets to carry the flint and shell scrapers. I hope you don't mind. We will need them to dig away the charred wood. A burning log can't be left while we come home to dinner. It might burn too much or set the forest on fire. We will take you on a boat ride when it is finished. Be a sweet sister and, please, bring us some lunch," coaxed Situ.

"Oh, I guess I will," said the girl. "I want to bring Koma some roasted muskrat and some stewed pumpkin. I might as well bring you some mush, Situ, at the same time."

Situ smiled at his little sister. She smiled back at him. Koma leaned over and caught a frog at the edge of the spring. "Look what I've got," he said.

He handed the frog to Situ, who knew just how to use it. Situ rubbed the tiny animal over his stomach in a circular motion; he sighed with relief. His stomach felt better. His people had taught him that it was possible for his own stomach ache to leave him and to go into the body of the frog.

"It is too bad for such a little animal to have such a big ache. Now it will really have something to croak about. You know, I think my head feels better, too." Situ gently turned the frog loose. It jumped into the spring. It did not act as if it had an ache.

By the early afternoon Ikwa felt better too. Back at the village she had filled a pot with meat and vegetables and another with mush. It was time for the one big meal of the day. Several women cooked it in huge pots for the whole village. Each woman who was head of a household brought a big bowl and took her family's share from the huge pots. Then the women served the men first and ate what was left. The cook always had a pot of corn meal for those who wanted it. The old people with bad teeth and the babies ate

44

*Ikwa's mother watches the races on the river.*

this mush. Ikwa hoped that the men wouldn't eat too much and that there would be enough for the women and children.

Now Ikwa was on her way to take food to the boys. In her hands she carried the pots of meat, vegetables, and mush. She had put her string bag over her shoulder in case she saw any wild plants she wanted to gather. Already it was full of smilax roots, like small potatoes, and some grasshoppers to roast. She heard the boys laugh as she came down the trail to the tree boat.

The two cousins were sitting by the boat carefully making dart points. Each boy had a tiny piece of flint in his hand. Each was carefully pressing the outer edges of the flint with a deer antler. The flint flaked where they pressed, and they were able to make two triangular-shaped sharp points.

"I know that my point is better than yours."

"Well my point is going to kill more animals. We certainly need to kill something if Ikwa is going to have a new apron. We can't dress her in a fish."

Ikwa knew that they hadn't found the answer to her problem, but she smiled and gave them the food. She even gave them a few of the grasshoppers to roast. They cooked them over the smoking center of the boat. Situ put a layer of clay on the outside of the boat to keep that part from burning. Then they made the fire hotter in the center.

Ikwa visited with the boys and helped scrape out the burned wood. As the sun began to show his colors to the world, Ikwa hastened back to the village. She did not want to be in the woods when the night spirits came out.

As soon as Ikwa got home she went to Inna's house. She and Inna untied the baby from the cradle board. He laughed and kicked and waved his arms. They gave him a bath. She watched him kick for a while, then carefully bound him back on the cradle board. Keeping his head bound caused it to grow flat in the back and a little pointed on top. These Indians thought that a pointed head was the prettiest-shaped head of all. Finally, Ikwa hung the baby's board on a peg in the house. She gave it a little push, and the baby was gently rocked to sleep.

Then Ikwa helped Inna bathe. She washed the little girl's neck and scrubbed behind her ears. She helped Inna unroll her straw mat on the sleeping platform. Then she told both children goodnight. As she started out the door, she turned and spoke to Inna, "Don't put the long stick on the fire. It will reach too close to the walls." Ikwa hated to leave the children alone, but her mother had told her to come home early. She went to her house and got in bed herself. She fell asleep right away.

24

*These houses belong to the families of Ikwa and Inna.*

# 6

# A Light in the Darkness—Fire!

A wiser girl lay sleeping that night. She slept soundly. She did not dream.

Ikwa, Ikwa, Ikwa, wake up! The alarm drum was sounding, "Thum, thum, thum, thum...." What was wrong?

Ikwa got up quickly and tied on her old apron. Smoke was choking her. She went outside. Inna's house was on fire. Flames were leaping high into the sky. The walls were smoking and cracking. The mud on the walls was being baked hard like pottery. The whole village was lighted by the flames of the burning house. Ikwa knew that the spirits of the dead were disturbed. They danced in the shadows when a building burned. Sometimes they took the form of an animal.

The dogs began to bark and whimper. The whole village was awake now. The friendly puppy began to howl. Was that the death howl? Did he smell the messenger of death? Had the messenger come to guide someone on the long journey to the spirit world? Where was Koma's baby brother? He was such a tiny boy, and he was still bound to his cradle board. Did Koma's little sister take him from the peg in the house where it hung? Where was little Inna? She was asleep in the house when the fire started. Did she get out? The house was burning too badly for anyone to go inside. The fire was too hot for anyone to go through the door. The walls were about to collapse. Ikwa's father and two other men had to hold the children's father to keep him from running into the flaming house to look for his little girl and baby boy. Were his children being burned to death? Was the fire god taking them for his own? Ikwa tried to see through the doorway. The god of fire filled her eyes and lungs with smoke. She had to back away from his great heat. Fear filled her heart.

Someone shouted, "Here comes the priest from the mound. He will know what to do. He will talk to angry spirits. Fire is the servant of the sun. The sun god is taking a sacrifice."

The old priest spoke, "Get all the water jars and pots in the village. Empty the gourds we use to store the corn and beans. Form a line to the river. Pass the water and the empty jars back and forth. We must wet the walls and the roof of the next house. We have to stop the fire before the whole village burns. The woods and fields are dry too. If we don't hurry the fire will spread and all of our crops will burn. Hurry! Hurry! Faster! Faster! Keep that water coming."

The priest began a magic chant to the gods. It had a strange, fast rhythm. The drum picked up its beat. A reed flute joined in. A chorus of voices chanted the words. Water jars passed in time to the strange tune. The fire god heard the music and liked it. He listened to the people for over an hour. The fire god did not eat the next house. He went to sleep instead. The fields, too, were safe. They would have food for winter. They would not have to live off the Eagle

Village or move to the Place of All Gods to work on the mounds this year in order to get enough to eat.

Ikwa's arms ached from passing the heavy jars. How she longed to rest. The village children had all quit. Ikwa was determined not to give up. She was going to act like a woman. She was not going to complain. Her eyes were red from the smoke. Her throat hurt and she coughed a dry cough.

Her father spoke, "Ikwa, my child, you have worked hard. The fire will sleep now. Go down to the spring. Wash your face in the cool water and get a drink. Be careful, watch out for snakes. Strange spirits are walking tonight. Take this jar and bring some spring water to the priest and the other people in line."

Ikwa was so tired and sad that tears ran from her smoke-reddened eyes. She could hardly see to watch for snakes as she went.

A tiny cry came from behind a bush. What made that noise? Ikwa stood still trying to see through her tears. She was afraid to move.

A weak voice whispered, "Ikwa. . . ."

Ikwa had heard this voice before. This wasn't the voice of a spirit. It was the voice of a little girl! And she had her brother on her back!

Something must have wakened the children. Ikwa thought of the children's dead mother. How foolish they had been to worry about the children. The spirits of the dead protect the living. The spirit of the children's mother had been in the house when the fire started.

Ikwa's voice rang out loud and clear, "Inna and the baby are here at the spring! The children are safe!"

The people nearest the spring heard the news. The good news traveled from one person to the next just like the

## 25

*The dead sleep beneath the clay floors of the houses.*

water pots. The chant of the priest changed into a joyful song. It was one of thanks. Ikwa felt a moment of happiness.

Little Inna sobbed, "Don't let them hurt me, Ikwa. I didn't mean to set the house on fire. I got cold and put one of the bigger logs on the fire. I didn't want the baby to get cold. I hid here because I don't want to be cut or scratched. No bad spirits are inside me. I'm so good." Then Inna started sobbing harder than ever.

This waked the baby up, and he started to scream. Ikwa lifted the baby's board and put it on her own back. She took the unhappy little girl into her arms. She swayed back and forth and gently rocked both children at the same time. She was quiet a moment trying to think of something to say to Inna. These thoughts went through her mind:

"Your own deeds are the spirits of life. They bring their own rewards and punishments. I wish that I could be scratched or cut and that all my badness and foolishness would be gone. I wish that life were as simple as that."

Then Ikwa spoke, "I know that you didn't mean to start the fire. I will tell them. Stop crying and let's go back to your father. I'll stay with you. Everything will be all right for you."

"Yes," she thought, "I'll stay with you. I will be the child who is left behind when the others go on the trip. Will everything ever be all right for me?"

## 26

*Ikwa's grandmother makes a basket to use in housebuilding. It will hold about 40 pounds of clay for the floor and walls.*

# 7

# A Change in Plans

Ikwa slept long after the howls of the priest had awakened the sun. The morning light revealed the ashes of one burned house and two other houses blackened from the smoke. Ikwa's grandmother and another woman were pushing sticks through the ashes to see if any of the household goods remained unburned.

Koma's father had launched a canoe at dawn and was traveling down the river. He was returning to his clan's home in the Eagle Village. He would bring his sisters and some of their family back with him to help build his new house. They would load his canoe with marriage gifts for Lowe's family. These would show how valuable his clan thought she was. Since Lowe was taking her dead sister's place as his wife, the wedding would take place in the Alligator Village. When the new house was finished, the old priest would come down from the mound. He would bring a stick lighted with the sacred fire from the temple. This would be used to light the fire in the new house. Then the bride and the groom and his children would move in together. The children would have a new mother.

Ikwa awakened that morning when her mother shook her. She felt the black, rough taste of smoke in her mouth. No wonder she ached. She had passed dozens of heavy water jugs the night before. She had shared her narrow sleeping platform with Inna. This platform was raised about four feet from the clay floor. Some Indians built their beds this high so that bugs and fleas couldn't hop on the sleepers from the ground. The smoke from the fire hearth kept the mosquitos out of the house. When two girls slept on this narrow shelf, one was in danger of falling. Ikwa and her mother would have to build another bed for Inna to use until her new house was finished.

"Get up, Ikwa," her mother said. "We have much work to do. I want you to weave a new grass mat for Inna while I cut small logs and cane for a platform. We have guests arriving too. Some of the Eagle women are coming to help with the housebuilding. I think that Noha's mother and sister may come. I especially want everything to look nice for them. Behave yourself, and please don't waste time daydreaming."

Ikwa spent the morning hunting the right kind of grass and reeds for the mat. She was in a bamboo thicket when she heard the dogs bark. She peeped through the leaves and saw eight strange women following Koma's father up the path. She stayed hidden. Even when the sun rose high in the sky, she did not go to get her lunch. She was too shy and too ashamed to meet the strangers in her dirty old apron. She crept down to a green glade by the spring to make the mat. The water running over the side of the spring made a little waterfall. The day was hot, and Ikwa let the water trickle on her bare feet. It felt good. She heard a drum sound in the distance. She wiggled her toes in the mud in time to the beat. Her busy fingers wove faster.

## 27

*Ikwa's people enjoyed wearing shell necklaces. On some of these were carved pictures of men playing games. The first two pictures show chunky players; the third shows a runner wearing a chunky stone around his neck.*

One of the strange women came down to the spring and spoke to her before she had time to run and hide. The woman was tall and stern looking. She was very clean and neat.

"You are Ikwa, aren't you? I have been looking for you. Your mother said that I might find you here. I am Rata, Noha's mother. Don't you hear the drums? They are calling everyone to the chunky games. I know that you must want to see them because Situ is playing. He usually wins, doesn't he? I hear that after the chunky stone is rolled, his spear is usually the one thrown closest to it. Come on, let's hurry to the plaza to watch."

Ikwa smiled and shyly answered, "It is most kind of you to look for me. Thank you. Yes, I want to watch Situ, but I must finish this mat. If I don't, Inna won't have a bed tonight. She was so upset last night. If I stop now, I might not have enough time to finish it later. Maybe I will get through in time to see the last of the contests."

Rata gave her a puzzled look and then asked another question, "Are you planning to dance tonight?"

"Yes, the other girls and I have been practicing for weeks. The priest is going to choose a new handmaiden tonight. I wish that he could choose all of us."

"Well, I will look for you in the plaza then." The older woman turned and started back in the direction of the sound of the drum.

Ikwa had no idea what Noha's mother was thinking. The woman had not smiled at all. Ikwa could hear the cheers and cries of the crowd at the game. She wished she could watch, but the mat kept her busy. Finally she finished the last row. She looked at her face in the spring. She tried to smooth her hair. The face pictured in the water did not smile at her. She started slowly back to the village.

28

The bed that Ikwa and her mother built for Inna. This bed was
used as a bench during the day when the weather was bad.
But since the house was dark and smoky, they liked to stay
outside as much as possible.

*When earth was taken out of the ground to make a mound, it left a hole. This hole filled with water and made a good fish pond. Live fish were kept here in a wicker fish trap.*

A loud cheer reminded her to hurry. She put her mat on Inna's newly made bed. She would get something to eat and then go to watch the last part of the games. It wouldn't matter now if the strangers saw her. Noha's mother had already seen how terrible she looked. She picked up an empty bowl and went to get some food from the big cooking pot. It was empty too. The fire under it had gone out. The puppy and one other dog were sleeping in the sun. They had a full, contented look.

"This is terrible. There should always be something to eat for the hunters who have missed meals and especially for the hungry baby. What will our guests think of us? Someone needs to go to the fields for more vegetables. But who will go? Everyone is in the plaza watching the games. I can't let the visitors know we have run out of food."

With a sigh Ikwa picked up a basket and started to walk toward the hot fields. She kicked the dust as she went. When she got to the field, she went to the blind, a small hut. Young boys stayed here each day to frighten away the deer and birds that came to eat the crops. The three boys in the blind agreed to get the vegetables and some sticks for the fire. Ikwa went to the pond to get some fish. Live fish were kept in willow fish traps at the water's edge. Situ and Koma had put some there last week. Ikwa took them out, got her stone knife, and cleaned them.

She and the little boys worked rapidly. The food was just beginning to boil when a ringing cheer was heard. The games were over. The Alligator women's honor was saved.

Ikwa was so tired that she didn't feel like eating now. She had tried and tried to get the fish smell off her hands. She had rubbed them almost raw on the sand at the river's edge. Still the smell lingered. She went into the house to get her only shell bracelet and her ceremonial paints. She put

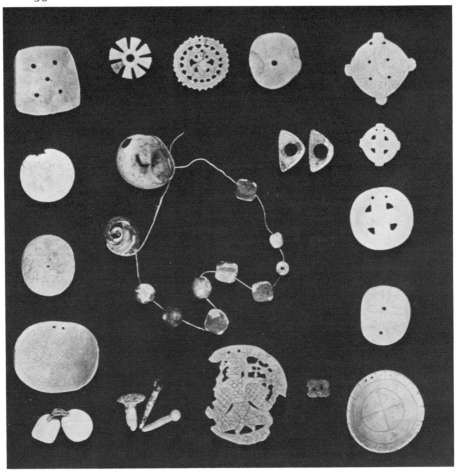

## 30

Koma and Situ and the girls enjoyed making and wearing jewelry. Many pieces show scenes and designs. Often these pieces are made of shell. Ear spools look like mushrooms and are made of shell, wood, or clay. A few are covered with a thin layer of beaten copper. These were put through a slit in the ear lobe. Some Indians wore shell beads. Others wore fresh-water pearls, which they found in mussel shells.

grease on her face and then patted on the powdered colors. Situ came in to get his feather cape and leg rattles for the dances. He had a big smile on his face.

"Will you help the champion chunky player with his paint? I never can get it on straight." He handed her his paint palette. Then his smile disappeared, and a look of pity came on the face she was painting.

"Ikwa, sometimes it is better for a young woman to be the second wife of an older man. A first wife can guide and help her. A man who is rich enough to have more than one wife is usually very important, like the important trader who came last week. His wives will travel many places and see many wonderful things."

Situ saw the puzzled look on Ikwa's face turn to one of horror. He started to say something else to her but changed his mind. He reached up and took down a beautiful shell necklace, which he had made for his future bride. He slipped this over his sister's head. Before Ikwa could say a word he ran out of the door. The dance drums sounded.

Ikwa moved as though she were in a daze. She didn't remember walking to the square. The drummers beat faster. The Indian maidens formed a line. Dancers followed the rhythm of the beat. Hands rose and fell, feet stamped the ground, and bodies swayed and bent.

The sun touched the horizon, and a cry went up from the crowd. The priest came out of the temple. He raised his arms toward the sun. His hand held the sacred mace, a symbol of power. Sinu, a pretty Indian girl about Ikwa's age, picked up a basket of vegetables and started climbing the mound. The crowd cheered. Ikwa knew then that Sinu had been chosen as the new handmaiden. Sinu would take the trip down the river to the Place of All Gods. Sinu's basket burned on top of the mound with a blaze of light. The priest sang a strange chant. Then the priest and the girl went into the temple together. The dancing in the square would continue until dawn.

Ikwa felt now that her whole life was dark like the sky. Her future looked black. Tears filled her eyes. She tried to blink them back.

Male dancers took the places of the Indian maidens in the square. Situ led the dancers. Ikwa walked over to little Inna, who had her sleeping brother on her back. Inna's eyes were closed, and her chin rested on her chest. Ikwa tenderly touched her. Inna's head jerked up and her eyes opened.

"Come, Inna, I'll put you and the baby to bed. I know you both are very tired."

She took the baby from Inna, and the three of them started back to the house. A tear escaped from Ikwa's eye and made a streak in her paint. When they got to the house, she bathed the baby and arranged him for the night. Then she helped the tired little girl climb up on the new mat on the new sleeping platform.

"Don't leave me, Ikwa, I'm afraid that this house might catch on fire too."

Ikwa looked at Inna, "I'll stay with you. Don't worry." She climbed on her own bed and closed her eyes. After a long time she fell asleep. In her dreams the same tattooed snake began to dance. The snake beat a stick in time to the rhythm of the drum. The snake kept coming closer and closer to her.

# 8

## A New Home

The week that followed was a busy one. Sometimes Ikwa thought of being married to the tattooed trader as a second wife. The thought was so horrible that Ikwa couldn't make herself ask anyone about it. She was afraid of the answer she would get. She imagined that everyone felt sorry for her. She thought that she could see pity in their eyes when they looked at her. She noticed that Noha's mother watched her.

But most of the time Ikwa kept as busy as she possibly could. When she was hard at work she was too busy to think of herself. When she thought of others and did things for them she did not think of her own troubles.

She worked hard on the new house. She continued to dig the holes for the poles that supported the side walls and roof. She dug even when the sun shone the hottest. She wouldn't stop weaving the framework of sticks, even though her fingers ached. The sticks were needed to support the mud on the side walls. At last, the house looked like a giant basket. Then Ikwa carried more mud for the side walls than any other girl in the village. She cut sage grass for the roof

## 31

*The frame of Inna's house is almost finished. It looks like a big upside-down basket.*

and separated it from the briers. She did not complain. Instead she taught little Inna the work songs she knew. She worked side by side with the Eagle women. She tried to make them feel welcome in her village.

At last the house was finished. The priest came down from the temple mound bringing a blazing stick to light a new fire. The brightness and warmth of the sun would light the new home. The Eagle women gave the gifts that they had brought to the Alligator Clan. Then the Eagle man took Lowe's hand. The two of them walked into their new home. They had become man and wife. Inna and the baby had a new mother.

All the other people were sitting around a fire in the plaza. Rata, Noha's mother, rose. She stood very straight and looked very solemn. She held up her hand to quiet the crowd:

"When I came here I had two jobs to do. One was a serious one and one, the happy one of building this house. The house is finished, and the new family is a good one. The ties between your people and my people are strengthened by this union. And now for my other job. . . .

"Last week a trader visited the Eagle Village. He brought with him the story of a foolish maiden. It was the story of a child who did not think before she acted. He told us the story of a child's mind, of a child who thought only of herself. He said, 'Her simple mind might never leave her body. Her body might grow but her mind might not.'

"This story was very distressing to us. We did not want to believe it. The trader showed us this apron as proof." Rata held up Ikwa's pretty new apron.

A murmer went through the crowd. Ikwa wanted to run and hide. But she was too frightened and embarrassed to move. Everyone was looking at her. Then Rata began to

32

*Koma congratulates his father and Lowe on their marriage.*

speak again:

"Noha, my son, is a fine young man of seventeen summers. He is a swift runner and a brave fighter. His bow shoots straight. He has killed the bear and the bobcat alone. He knows the secrets of the woods. He is wise beyond his years. Any woman would be proud to be his wife. My clan felt that only the finest maiden should be chosen for him.

"The trader offered to marry this foolish girl, who had been promised to Noha. He said that his first wife might be able to beat some sense into her. He said that the foolish one was strong. She could carry his trade goods on her back and paddle his canoe. The trader offered to marry this girl in Noha's place if Noha would give him four bear hides as a marriage gift. He said that the Alligator Clan would be proud to have one of its members married to an important trader."

The crowd gasped. Rata raised her hand for silence again:

"I told you that my son was wise beyond his years. This was his answer to the trader: 'It is not wise to look at something only through the eyes of a stranger. Often there are things which another does not wish you to see. The only trade which I will make today is that of my bear claw necklace and one bear hide for that apron which you have. Stop here on your next trip down the river, and we will talk again.' "

Noha's mother walked over to Ikwa with the garment. She continued speaking:

"On this trip I have been Noha's eyes, and this is what I have seen: A maiden who is kind and loving to two motherless children. She will make a good mother. I have seen a girl who knows disappointment, but who still knows how to sing. I have seen a woman who knows that honor is important and that an empty pot must be filled. I know why

69

she smelled like fish at the dances. A small boy told me the story of some dogs who had a feast. Ikwa knows that an empty pot must be filled. She has put honor and work ahead of her own pleasure. This young woman does not brag or complain. She is willing to work hard for others, and she does not stop until her tasks are finished.

"I see now that Ikwa's foolish trade was her last act as a child. The new spirit of a woman has driven away the foolish spirit.

"Ikwa, here is the apron, which Noha sent to you. I give it now to his future bride. Wear your new clothes proudly, for he will be proud of you. Remember that next year you will travel to the Place of All Gods to become the wife of a kind, handsome young man."

The spirit of joy was inside Ikwa, now a young woman. She stepped forward, and her future mother-in-law helped her tie on her new clothes.

# acknowledgments

I would like to acknowledge my appreciation to some of the experts who have so kindly assisted me, especially my colleagues in the Anthropology Department of The University of Alabama: David L. DeJarnette, Professor of Anthropology and Curator of Mound State Monument, who first instilled in me a love of Southeastern Archaeology; Dr. A. T. Hansen, social anthropologist, who taught me how people live together in groups; Dr. John A. Walthall, who checked the accuracy of my material; and Dr. C. Earle Smith and Dr. Paul H. Nesbitt, who assisted in a number of ways. Professor William Otha Hopper allowed me to attend his creative writing courses while I was preparing this manuscript, and Valerie Scarritt gave me invaluable editorial assistance.

Persons providing illustrations include: Thomas H. DeJarnette, Preparator of the Museum of Natural History, The University of Alabama, who created many of the excellent dioramas and village scenes, which may be viewed at Mound State Monument, Moundville, Alabama (2, 5, 8, 9, 11, 14, 15, 25, 32), and his son, Don, who made some of the photographs (9, 29). Other photographs (cover, 7, 10, 16, 22, 30) were made by the late Joseph Barrett; while others (2, 5, 8, 11, 14, 15, 25, 32) were supplied by Andrew S. Russell, Photographic Editor, and Randy Satterfield (4), Office of Informational Services, The University of Alabama, which owns the original photographs.

Original drawings were prepared by Nina Ross Gessler, who patterned the tattoos, clothing, and hair styles in Picture 13 after engravings of Theodor de Bry. The dog was patterned after skeletal material found by David Chase, Auburn University, and a description by Thomas Hariot, 1588. In Picture 17 the snake in the treetop is based upon a design found at Spiro, Oklahoma; the snakes around Ikwa are pictured on the rattlesnake disc at Moundville, Alabama; while the serpent in the lower left hand corner is patterned after a design on a shell gorget found in Arkansas. Dan Bollman copied the designs (27) which were found on conch shell gorgets. The first was found in Perry County, Missouri, the second in Eddyville, Kentucky, and the third in Spiro, Oklahoma. The third can be seen at the Museum of the American Indian, Heye Foundation, New York. The engravings and maps are reproduced through the courtesy of Dr. Herman Viola of the Smithsonian Institution, Bureau of American Ethnology, and are as follows:

1. Map of Mound Locations in the Eastern United States (reproduced from *The Mound Builders* by Henry Clay Shetrone, fig. 8).

19. A map of natural resources used by the Indians in the Southeast (John R. Swanton (1946), map 13, face p. 254).

Illustrations 6 and 18 are from engravings by Theodor de Bry after the paintings by Jacques le Moyne de Morgues.

20. From an engraving by Theodor de Bry after a water color by John White (1587). The subjects were witnessed by White on the Coastal Area of North Carolina.

23. From an engraving by Theodor de Bry after the painting by John White (1590) of Indians in Virginia.

The headdress (3) is one which was reproduced by archaeologists at Etowah Mounds Archaeological Area, Cartersville, Georgia, where I was assisted by L. Henry Tumlin. Dr. Lewis H. Larson, Jr., provided this photograph (3) and also the one of the cloth (12) through the courtesy of the Historic Preservation Section, Georgia Department of Natural Resources.

Merit Clements Lee of the Audio-Visual Aids Department, The University of Alabama, gave me valuable suggestions on numerous occasions, and members of The University of Alabama Press helped me in many ways.

Lastly, I would like to thank the Cherokees at Tsa-La-Gi, Tahlequah, Oklahoma, who allowed me to photograph their handiwork showing the way in which their ancestors lived (Frontis, 21, 26, 28, 31); and the Indian peoples at Anadarko, Oklahoma (24), and elsewhere, who have so graciously received me at reservations in Mississippi, Oklahoma, North Carolina, and Arizona and whose archaeological sites I have visited throughout the Southeast.